FOSSIL FINDS

Dinosaurs first roamed Earth at the beginning of the Mesozoic era, more than **250 MILLION YEARS AGO.** For the next 185 million years, they lived and thrived in an amazing prehistoric environment—until a catastrophic mass extinction wiped them out.

How can we tell what dinosaurs looked like? And how do we know about the ways they interacted with each other?

FOSSILS—remains preserved from a past geologic age—give scientists the answers to many of these questions, and dinosaur teeth hold especially important clues to how these animals lived.

Come and peer inside the jaws of dinosaurs, from little Coelophysis to towering Apatosaurus and terrifying T. rex, and see what you can discover about the lives of these fascinating and fearsome creatures.

THE FOSSIL EVIDENCE

More than 1,000 species of dinosaurs have been discovered so far through fossil finds worldwide. Thanks to these remains, scientists are able to determine an amazing amount of information.

SOLVING CLUES

Using just a few pieces of bone, scientists can tell how big an animal was and what it might have looked like. For example, footprints and leg bones hold answers to how fast a dinosaur could run, and scientists can also figure out the size of a dinosaur's brain by examining its skull. Computer models based on these fossils can also be created to explore the answers to questions such as how fast Diplodocus could whip its tail, or how Allosaurus ate its meals.

DENTAL RECORDS

Teeth are more common than other fossils and are very valuable clues to discovering how dinosaurs lived. In fact, some dinosaurs like meat-eater Deinodon are known only because of their teeth! Why are there so many fossils of teeth? Firstly, teeth fossilize more easily than bone or other materials. Secondly, the jaws of some types of dinosaur held rows of replacement teeth. Whenever a tooth fell out another one moved in to take its place, and these dinosaurs lost many teeth throughout their lifetime.

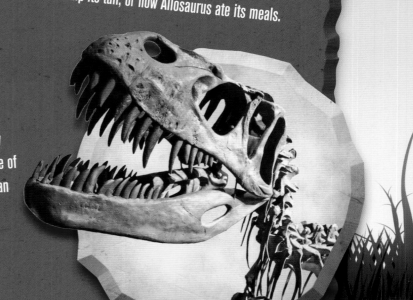

SINK YOUR TEETH INTO
DINOSAURS!

SCHOLASTIC

CONTENTS

WHAT'S FOR LUNCH?

Based on the shape and size of a fossilized tooth, we can put together a picture of the dinosaur's diet.

MEAT-EATERS often had sharp, knife-like teeth that helped them wound prey by slashing, or curved teeth that could help them grip slippery or wriggly prey.

PLANT-EATERS usually had beaks or thin, rake-like teeth for clipping and stripping leaves, or flat, ridged teeth for grinding plants.

BIG TEETH FOR A BIG APPETITE

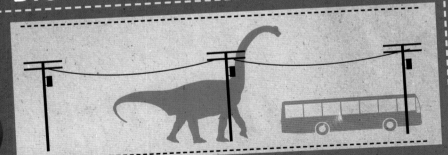

about 45 feet (13.7 m)

Many dinosaurs were big—**REALLY BIG!** Some of the dinosaurs you'll read about in this book were as long as city buses, or as tall as telephone poles. To get that big, they probably had to eat constantly.

SAUROPODS: Scientists think these large plant-eating dinosaurs could have consumed more than 100,000 calories a day. We'd have to eat 3,333 cups of broccoli to consume that many calories!

THEROPODS: Big meat-eaters like Tyrannosaurus rex could chomp more than 500 pounds (227 kg) of meat in one bite.

DINOSAUR
TYRANNOSAURUS REX

PRONUNCIATION: TIE-RAN-OH-SORE-USS RECKS

FOSSIL FILE 1

T. rex had a mouthful of nearly 60 banana-shaped teeth, each one about 12 inches (30.5 cm) long. Some scientists think this meat-eater actively preyed on small and medium-sized dinosaurs, as well as weaker large dinosaurs.

DINOSTATS!

NAME MEANS: TYRANT LIZARD KING

SIZE: 43 FEET *(13 M)* IN LENGTH, 20 FEET *(6 M)* TALL

YIKES!!!

AVG HUMAN:
5 FT. 8 IN. (1.72 M)

WEIGHT: 14,000 POUNDS *(6,350 KG)*

PERIOD: LATE CRETACEOUS, 85–65 MILLION YEARS AGO

FOSSILS LOCATED: NORTH AMERICA: FROM MEXICO TO CANADA

LIZARD KING

Hundreds of T. rex fossils have been discovered, including a fossilized Hadrosaur with a T. rex tooth stuck in its healed bone. This means that the Hadrosaur survived the attack—and that the T. rex lost a tooth! Some scientists think T. rex was a scavenger, rather than a predator, because of its small arms and little eyes. Either way, T. rex definitely ate Triceratops: fossilized T. rex droppings have contained bits of Triceratops bone.

DINOSAUR
APATOSAURUS

PRONUNCIATION: ah–PAH–tow–SORE–us

Apatosaurus teeth are often described as being like pencils. Thin and blunt, these teeth probably didn't help Apatosaurus chew. Scientists think that this dinosaur, like Barosaurus and many of its fellow large sauropods, may have swallowed stones to help it grind up and digest food.

DINOSTATS!

NAME MEANS: FALSE LIZARD

SIZE: 75 FEET *(23 M)* IN LENGTH, 30 FEET *(9 M)* TALL

AVG HUMAN:
5 FT. 8 IN. (1.72 M)

WEIGHT: 40,000–75,000 POUNDS *(18,143–34,019 KG)*

PERIOD: LATE JURASSIC, 154–150 MILLION YEARS AGO

FOSSILS LOCATED: NORTH AMERICA: UNITED STATES

LOUISE, THE DINO

Apatosaurus's scientific name, *Apatosaurus louisae*, comes from Louise Carnegie, wife of Andrew Carnegie, a wealthy industrialist who funded many excavations in the early 1900s. The most complete Apatosaurus skeleton includes an intact skull and is on display at the Carnegie Museum of Natural History in Pittsburgh, Pennsylvania. This plant-eater was huge: a recently uncovered thighbone stands 6 feet (1.8 m) tall, just a few inches larger than an average male human.

DINOSAUR
EUOPLOCEPHALUS

PRONUNCIATION: YOO-OH-PLO-SEF-AH-LUSS

FOSSIL FILE ③

An herbivore, Euoplocephalus had about 40 small teeth arranged in rows in its mouth. As the dinosaur chewed, the teeth would grind up the cycads, ferns, and other low-growing plants that made up its diet.

DINOSTATS!

NAME MEANS: WELL-ARMORED HEAD

SIZE: 20 FEET (7 M) IN LENGTH, 6.5 FEET (2 M) TALL

UH OH...

AVG HUMAN:
5 FT. 8 IN. (1.72 M)

WEIGHT: 4,000 POUNDS (1,814 KG)

PERIOD: LATE CRETACEOUS, 99–65 MILLION YEARS AGO

FOSSILS LOCATED: NORTH AMERICA: CANADA AND UNITED STATES

ARMORED WARRIOR

Like its fellow Ankylosauria (armored dinosaurs), Euoplocephalus resembled a big turtle covered with protective spikes and bony plates—even on its eyelids. Although scientists deduce what most dinosaurs looked like based on bits and pieces of fossilized skeletons, dozens of Euoplocephalus fossils have been found, including some nearly complete skeletons with their armor still in place. This means we know almost exactly what they looked like.

DINOSAUR
VELOCIRAPTOR

PRONUNCIATION: VEH-LOSS-ih-RAP-tor

FOSSIL FILE 4

Velociraptors' jaws were lined with about 15 curved, knife-like teeth on each side. Razor-sharp, they were perfect for hooking into prey and chomping. Fossil evidence suggests that Velociraptors were likely both scavengers and active predators.

DINOSTATS!

NAME MEANS: FAST ROBBER

SIZE: 6 FEET *(1.8 M)* IN LENGTH, 2.5 FEET *(0.7 M)* TALL

ARGH!!!

AVG HUMAN: 5 FT. 8 IN. *(1.72 M)*

WEIGHT: 50–100 POUNDS *(23–45 KG)*

PERIOD: LATE CRETACEOUS, 75–71 MILLION YEARS AGO

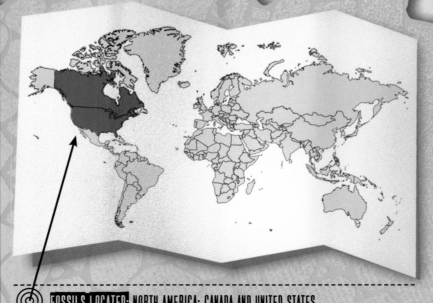

FOSSILS LOCATED: NORTH AMERICA: CANADA AND UNITED STATES

HUNGRY HUNTER

Velociraptors weren't large, but they were deadly. With sharp teeth and a long, 3.5-inch (9-cm) claw on the middle toe of each foot, they were able to slash and grasp prey. A large brain in relation to its body size suggests it was intelligent, with good hearing, sight, and smell—keen senses for hunting. Fast and nimble, Velociraptors could run at speeds of up to 25 mph (40 kph), easily outpacing their victims.

DINOSAUR
MAJUNGASAURUS

PRONUNCIATION: MAH-JUNG-AH-SORE-USS

FOSSIL FILE 5

Majungasaurus had a shorter, rounder jaw than other big dinosaur predators. Because of this, and because of the shape of its teeth, Majungasaurus likely killed its prey by clamping down in a bite and holding, rather than just slashing and tearing at flesh.

DINOSTATS!

NAME MEANS: MADAGASCAN LIZARD

SIZE: 20 FEET *(6 M)* IN LENGTH, 11.5 FEET *(3.5 M)* TALL

YIKES!!!

AVG HUMAN:
5 FT. 8 IN. (1.72 M)

WEIGHT: 2,400 POUNDS *(1,088 KG)*

PERIOD: LATE CRETACEOUS, 70–65 MILLION YEARS AGO

FOSSILS LOCATED: AFRICA: MADAGASCAR

CANNIBAL LIZARD?

Majungasaurus sported a small, single horn on its head. Though it walked on two powerful legs, Majungasaurus had two stubby arms, with four nubby clawless fingers. Some scientists think its arms were completely useless and may have just hung there. Fossilized Majungasaurus bones have been found with teeth marks that match the bite of other Majungasauruses—suggesting these dinosaurs might have preyed on their own species!

DINOSAUR
SARCOSUCHUS

PRONUNCIATION: SAR-KO-SOOK-USS

FOSSIL FILE ... 6

Sarcosuchus had about 100 teeth in its massive 6-foot-long (1.8-m) jaws. Sarcosuchus probably ate turtles and fish, like modern crocodiles do. But it also likely attacked and ate dinosaurs that came too close.

DINOSTATS!

NAME MEANS: FLESH CROCODILE

SIZE: 40 FEET (12 M) IN LENGTH, 12 FEET (3.6 M) TALL

RUN!!!

AVG HUMAN:
5 FT. 8 IN. (1.72 M)

WEIGHT: 17,500 POUNDS (7,937 KG)

PERIOD: CRETACEOUS, 112–110 MILLION YEARS AGO

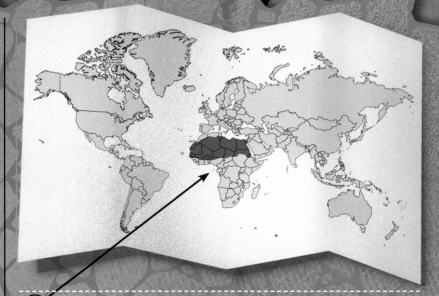

FOSSILS LOCATED: AFRICA: SAHARA DESERT

SUPER CROC

Sarcosuchus wasn't technically a dinosaur: it was a prehistoric crocodilian. These early reptiles were similar to today's alligators and crocodiles, but nearly twice the size! About the length of a school bus, Sarcosuchus lived near the riverbanks that once covered the Sahara Desert. Sarcosuchus had a unique bulge on the end of its snout that may have enhanced its sense of smell, attracted mates, or helped the animal make sounds to communicate with fellow super crocs.

DINOSAUR
HERRERASAURUS

PRONUNCIATION: HER-RARE-UH-SORE-USS

Herrerasaurus's long teeth turn toward the back of its jaws, and would have allowed it to grasp and hold onto struggling prey, likely small herbivores. It also had a hinged jaw that gave it a big bite.

DINOSTATS!

NAME MEANS: HERRERA'S LIZARD

SIZE: 15 FEET *(4.5 M)* IN LENGTH, 3.5 FEET *(1 M)* TALL

AVG HUMAN:
5 FT. 8 IN. (1.72 M)

WEIGHT: 450 POUNDS *(204 KG)*

PERIOD: TRIASSIC, 230–220 MILLION YEARS AGO

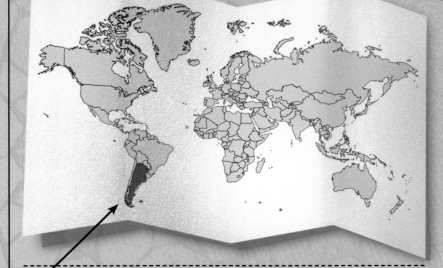

FOSSILS LOCATED: SOUTH AMERICA: ARGENTINA

THE FIRST PREDATOR

One of the very first dinosaurs, and the earliest known meat-eating dinosaur, Herrerasaurus was a top predator of the Triassic age, when dinosaurs were still rare. Herrerasaurus ran on powerful back legs and had strong hands with three long-clawed fingers, which scientists think it used to grasp and rip at prey. This carnivore was named after farmer Victor Herrera, who uncovered the first Herrerasaurus bones in the 1960s.

DINOSAUR

SPINOSAURUS

PRONUNCIATION: SPY-no-SORE-uss

FOSSIL FILE 8

Spinosaurus's head was 6 feet (1.8 m) long, with huge jaws. It had a mouthful of sharp, straight teeth, perfect for snaring big slippery fish—imagine a modern-day crocodile's jaws, only much, much bigger.

DINOSTATS!

NAME MEANS: SPINE LIZARD

SIZE: 56 FEET (17 M) IN LENGTH, 22 FEET (7 M) TALL

YIKES!!!

AVG HUMAN:
5 FT. 8 IN. (1.72 M)

WEIGHT: 14,000 POUNDS (6,350 KG)

PERIOD: MIDDLE CRETACEOUS, 112–97 MILLION YEARS AGO

FOSSILS LOCATED: AFRICA

DINO SWIMMER

Spinosaurus is named for the tall spikes down its back. They supported a huge sail, which may have helped the animal regulate its body temperature. It was the largest meat-eater ever on land, even bigger than T. rex, but recent fossil evidence shows that Spinosaurus was a water dinosaur, too—the first swimming dinosaur ever discovered. Fossils of this monstrous predator have been found in the Sahara Desert, which was marshy swampland and watershed during the Middle Cretaceous period.

DINOSAUR
DILOPHOSAURUS

PRONUNCIATION: DI-LO-FO-SORE-US

FOSSIL FILE

Dilophosaurus had about 30 sharp, pointy teeth—a few of which also had knife-like edges. The teeth got smaller toward the front of the jaw, where Dilophosaurus skulls have a gap. Dilophosaurus's teeth were thin at the bottom, which suggests they broke off easily.

DINOSTATS!

NAME MEANS: DOUBLE-CRESTED LIZARD

SIZE: 23 FEET *(7 M)* IN LENGTH, 8 FEET *(2.5 M)* TALL

HELP!!!

AVG WOMAN:
5 FT. 4 IN. *(1.62 M)*

WEIGHT: 1,100 POUNDS *(499 KG)*

PERIOD: EARLY JURASSIC, 200–190 MILLION YEARS AGO

FOSSILS LOCATED: NORTH AMERICA: SOUTHWESTERN UNITED STATES

PACK HUNTERS?

Dilophosaurus is named for the two thin, bony crests at the top of its skull. It had long, sharp claws, a movable thumb, and strong legs. Some scientists think this dinosaur used its hands and feet to slash and claw prey rather than biting it with its weak jaws. Dilophosaurus skeletons have been discovered near each other, leading scientists to believe that these dinosaurs may have hunted in packs.

DINOSAUR
PTERANODON

PRONUNCIATION: TER-RAN-OH-DON

FOSSIL FILE 10

Pteranodon's long, pointed beak ended in a sharp tip. But it didn't contain any teeth at all! This means that Pteranodon probably swallowed its prey—most likely fish—whole, similar to the way seabirds eat today.

DINOSTATS!

NAME MEANS: WINGED AND TOOTHLESS

SIZE: 25–33 FEET (7.6–10 M) WING TO WING, 6 FEET (1.8 M) TALL

CESSNA WINGSPAN: 36 FT. (10.9 M)

WEIGHT: UNKNOWN

PERIOD: CRETACEOUS, 89–70 MILLION YEARS AGO

FOSSILS LOCATED: NORTH AMERICA: UNITED STATES; EUROPE: ENGLAND

THREAT FROM ABOVE

Not technically a dinosaur, Pteranodon was the largest of a type of flying reptile known as a Pterosaur. Pteranodon's impressive wingspan was about the size of a small plane and is the biggest wingspan of any flying animal discovered to date. Pteranodon probably spent much of its time soaring over the water in search of prey, swooping down into the water to attack when it spotted a fish.

DINOSAUR
DIPLODOCUS

PRONUNCIATION: DI-PLOD-OH-KUSS

FOSSIL FILE 11

Diplodocus had about 40 thin teeth, grouped toward the front of its jaws, good for stripping leaves. Diplodocus's teeth were replaced about once a month: old teeth fell out and new ones would move into place. This prevented the teeth from wearing down due to Diplodocus's constant eating.

DINOSTATS!

NAME MEANS: DOUBLE BEAM

SIZE: 82 FEET *(25 M)* IN LENGTH, 46 FEET *(14 M)* TALL

WHOA!!!

AVG HUMAN:
5 FT. 8 IN. (1.72 M)

WEIGHT: 14,000 POUNDS *(6,350 KG)*

PERIOD: JURASSIC, 155–145 MILLION YEARS AGO

FOSSILS LOCATED: NORTH AMERICA: FROM MEXICO TO CANADA

A WHALE OF A TAIL!

Diplodocus's tail was a mighty 45 feet (13.7 m) long, about the length of a humpback whale. Scientists think Diplodocus may have swung its tail like a whip, with the tip reaching speeds of more than 750 mph (1,200 kph). This would have created a sound like a cannon blast to scare away predators. Usually, Diplodocus's tail acted as a counterbalance to its long neck while it grazed for food.

DINOSAUR
STEGOSAURUS

PRONUNCIATION: STEG-OH-SORE-USS

FOSSIL FILE

Stegosaurus's bony beak helped it pluck ferns, moss, fruit, palm-like cycads, and other Jurassic plants. It ground up the plant material by chewing with its small, thin teeth. Based on the size of its head and jaws, scientists think that Stegosaurus had a surprisingly weak bite: a modern dog could probably chomp harder.

DINOSTATS!

NAME MEANS: ROOF LIZARD

SIZE: 30 FEET (9 M) IN LENGTH, 12 FEET (3.6 M) TALL

WANT A TREAT?

AVG MAN:
5 FT. 10 IN. (1.78 M)

WEIGHT: 6,800 POUNDS (3,084 KG)

PERIOD: LATE JURASSIC, 150–144 MILLION YEARS AGO

FOSSILS LOCATED: NORTH AMERICA: SOUTHWESTERN UNITED STATES; EUROPE: PORTUGAL

ARMORED WARRIOR

Stegosaurus stands out thanks to the row of huge plates—some almost 2 feet (0.6 m) tall—along its back. Too thin to protect it against predators, the plates were probably used to attract mates. Scientists think it swung its spiked tail quickly to strike attackers. One Allosaurus fossil has a hole in its tailbone about the same size and shape as a stegosaurus tail spike. Ouch!

DINOSAUR
COMPSOGNATHUS

PRONUNCIATION: COMP-SOG-NAY-THUSS

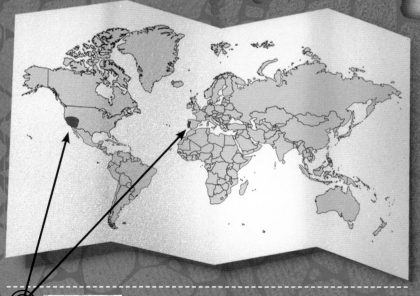

FOSSIL FILE 13

This dinosaur was named for its thin jawbone, which some scientists thought was pretty! These elegant jaws held small, sharp teeth that helped Compsognathus snatch up its favorite prey: small mammals and lizards, as well as insects.

DINOSTATS!

NAME MEANS: ELEGANT JAW

SIZE: 4 FEET (1.2 M) IN LENGTH, 2 FEET (0.6 M) TALL

KINDA CUTE?!

AVG MAN:
5 FT. 10 IN. (1.78 M)

WEIGHT: 10 POUNDS (4.5 KG)

PERIOD: LATE JURASSIC, 161–146 MILLION YEARS AGO

FOSSILS LOCATED: NORTH AMERICA: SOUTHWESTERN UNITED STATES; EUROPE: PORTUGAL

SMALL AND DEADLY

Although Compsognathus was bird-sized, it was not the tiniest dinosaur—that title goes to crow-sized Microraptor. Compsognathus had bird-like behavior, too. It laid its eggs in a nest and had spiky feathers on its body. But don't be fooled. It was a highly skilled predator. Compsognathus's large eyes, quick speed, estimated at 40 miles per hour (64 kph), and intelligence (thanks to a large brain-to-body ratio) made it a great hunter.

DINOSAUR
GIGANOTOSAURUS

PRONUNCIATION: JI-GA-NO-TOW-SORE-US

FOSSIL FILE

14

Not many Giganotosaurus fossils have been found. But among them is a nearly complete skull, which includes 8-inch-long (20.3-cm-long) sharp teeth, which means Giganotosaurus was able to slice into prey.

DINOSTATS!

NAME MEANS: GIANT SOUTHERN LIZARD

SIZE: 41 FEET (12.5 M) IN LENGTH, 16.5 FEET (5 M) TALL

YIKES!!!

AVG HUMAN: 5 FT. 8 IN. (1.72 M)

WEIGHT: 20,000 POUNDS (9,071 KG)

PERIOD: EARLY CRETACEOUS, 100–95 MILLION YEARS AGO

FOSSILS LOCATED: SOUTH AMERICA: ARGENTINA

LOOK FAMILIAR?

Giganotosaurus has a close lookalike: Tyrannosaurus rex. Bigger than T. rex and with three clawed fingers rather than two, Giganotosaurus roamed Earth alongside huge plant-eating dinosaurs. Unlike some other large theropods, which scientists think were scavengers, Giganotosaurus may have been able to actively hunt, attack, and kill gigantic sauropods. Fossilized remains of Argentinosaurus—one of the largest land animals ever, and weighing nearly 10 times as much as Giganotosaurus—have been found near this predator.

DINOSAUR
BAROSAURUS

PRONUNCIATION: BARE-OH-SORE-US

FOSSIL FILE

15

A Barosaurus skull has yet to be found, so we don't know for sure what its teeth looked like. But Barosaurus shares many features of other large sauropods, so it's likely that its teeth were similar to those of Apatosaurus or Diplodocus: long and peg-like, and ideal for stripping leaves from plants.

DINOSTATS!

NAME MEANS: HEAVY LIZARD

SIZE: 80 FEET *(24 M)* IN LENGTH, 40 FEET *(12 M)* TALL

BUS LENGTH:
37 FT. **(11.27 M)**

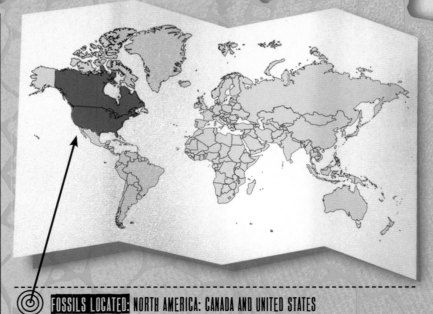

WEIGHT: 500,000 POUNDS *(226,796 KG)*

PERIOD: LATE JURASSIC, 155–145 MILLION YEARS AGO

FOSSILS LOCATED: NORTH AMERICA: CANADA AND UNITED STATES

STONY STOMACH

Barosaurus was a large plant-eating dinosaur similar to Diplodocus, but with a longer neck and a shorter tail. Not many Barosaurus fossils have been discovered, but those that have include some interesting details. For example, one fossil includes an imprint of what looks like tough and bumpy skin. Another Barosaurus skeleton shows that the animal's stomach contained gastroliths, stones that an animal swallows to help it grind up food.

DINOSAUR
CORYTHOSAURUS

PRONUNCIATION: CORE-ITH-OH-SORE-US

FOSSIL FILE 16

Corythosaurus was a type of duck-billed dinosaur also known as a Hadrosaur. A plant-eater, its bill had no teeth. Instead it had cheek teeth—blunt, fan-shaped teeth toward the back of its jaws. Numbering in the hundreds, these cheek teeth ground up food much like human molars do.

DINOSTATS!

NAME MEANS: HELMET LIZARD

SIZE: 21 FEET (6.4 M) IN LENGTH, 21 FEET (6.4 M) TALL

WANT A TREAT?

AVG HUMAN:
5 FT. 8 IN. (1.72 M)

WEIGHT: 8,860 POUNDS (4,019 KG)

PERIOD: LATE CRETACEOUS, 80–75 MILLION YEARS AGO

FOSSILS LOCATED: NORTH AMERICA: CANADA

HONKING HELMET

The special rounded crest atop Corythosaurus's head, often called a helmet, held a complex structure of tubes that connected to the animal's nostrils. The exact purpose of these tubes remains unclear, but some scientists think Corythosaurus could blow through them to make loud toots or honks to communicate with other dinosaurs or to warn of predators.

DINOSAUR
KRONOSAURUS

PRONUNCIATION: CROW–NO–SORE–USS

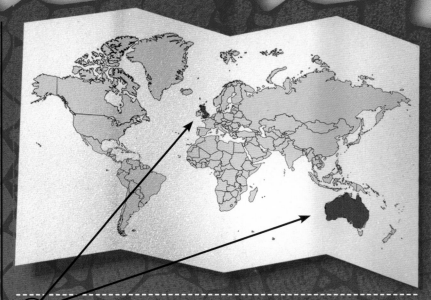

FOSSIL FILE 17

In 1899, a lower jaw and some large teeth were found: the first fossil discovery of Kronosaurus. Kronosaurus's teeth sat deep in its jaws, measuring about 1 foot (30 cm) in length from tip to root. These sharp chompers were ideal for tearing flesh from large fish, turtles, Ichthyosaurs, and maybe even another Kronosaurus.

DINOSTATS!

NAME MEANS: TITAN LIZARD

SIZE: 30–40 FEET *(9–12 M)* IN LENGTH, HEIGHT UNKNOWN

AVG HUMAN:
5 FT. 8 IN. (1.72 M)

WEIGHT: 12,000 POUNDS *(5,440 KG)*

PERIOD: EARLY CRETACEOUS, 110 MILLION YEARS AGO

FOSSILS LOCATED: EUROPE: ENGLAND; AUSTRALIA

SWIMMING MONSTER

Kronosaurus wasn't a dinosaur, but a type of sea-dwelling reptile known as a Pliosaur. Pliosaurs had short necks and big heads—about 6 feet (1.8 m) long—complete with big jaws. Kronosaurus used its four flippers to move through the water, swimming like a modern-day sea lion. Fossils show it had a large rib cage that probably housed equally large lungs and allowed this reptile to stay underwater for long periods.

COELOPHYSIS

PRONUNCIATION: SEE-LOW-FIE-SUSS

FOSSIL FILE 18

Coelophysis's long, thin jaws were lined with more than 100 small, sharp, and serrated teeth. Coupled with its claws, these teeth helped Coelophysis snatch and grasp prey.

DINOSTATS!

NAME MEANS: HOLLOW BONES

SIZE: 6 FEET *(1.8 M)* IN LENGTH, 6.5 FEET *(2 M)* TALL

AVG HUMAN:
5 FT. 8 IN. (1.72 M)

WEIGHT: 45 POUNDS *(20 KG)*

PERIOD: LATE TRIASSIC, 225–220 MILLION YEARS AGO

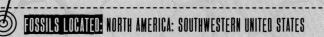

FOSSILS LOCATED: NORTH AMERICA: SOUTHWESTERN UNITED STATES

PACK HUNTER

With its thin body, long tail, and narrow head, this slim dinosaur was lightweight and streamlined, able to chase down the quick-moving lizards and small mammals it preyed upon. Coelophysis remains were involved in one of the most famous fossil finds: archaeologists in New Mexico uncovered hundreds of Coelophysis skeletons in one fossil bed. Scientists suspect this dinosaur was a pack hunter, and this particular pack was killed together by a flash flood or other disaster.

DINOSAUR
ALLOSAURUS

PRONUNCIATION: AL-low-SORE-uss

FOSSIL FILE 19

Allosaurus had a mouthful of about 30 sharp teeth, which it lost and replaced throughout its life. Four inches (10 cm) long and on the sides of its jaws, they curved backward and could hook into flesh when the dinosaur would bite. It's likely that Allosaurus never chewed its food, just gulped down chunks of flesh.

DINOSTATS!

NAME MEANS: DIFFERENT LIZARD

SIZE: 40 FEET *(12 M)* IN LENGTH, 16 FEET *(4.8 M)* TALL

YIKES!!!

AVG HUMAN:
5 FT. 8 IN. *(1.72 M)*

WEIGHT: 3,200 POUNDS *(1,450 KG)*

PERIOD: JURASSIC, 155–144 MILLION YEARS AGO

FOSSILS LOCATED: NORTH AMERICA: SOUTHWESTERN UNITED STATES, AS WELL AS MONTANA AND WYOMING

JURASSIC ATTACK

With knife-like teeth, sharp claws, and powerful legs, this meat-eater was a top predator. Though Allosaurus's arms were on the short side, they were strong compared to most meat-eaters' and could be used in attack on prey such as Stegosaurus and Diplodocus. Computer simulations created from Allosaurus skeletons show that it could move its head and neck quickly and precisely, allowing it to strip flesh off its prey.

DINOSAUR
TRICERATOPS

PRONUNCIATION: TRY-SER-AH-TOPS

Triceratops had a large beak and mouth rimmed with tightly spaced teeth. Its teeth acted like garden shears, clipping through tough plants. Like sharks today, Triceratops's jaws were lined with replacement teeth. Whenever one fell out or wore out, another moved into its place.

DINOSTATS!

NAME MEANS: THREE-HORNED FACE

SIZE: 30 FEET (9 M) IN LENGTH, 10 FEET (3 M) TALL

EEEEP!

AVG HUMAN:
5 FT. 8 IN. (1.72 M)

WEIGHT: 19,800 POUNDS (9,000 KG)

PERIOD: LATE CRETACEOUS, 72–65 MILLION YEARS AGO

FOSSILS LOCATED: NORTH AMERICA: WESTERN UNITED STATES AND CANADA

HELPFUL HORNS

Named after its three horns—which could grow up to 3 feet (0.9 m)—Triceratops was one of the last dinosaurs alive before the mass extinction. Its 8-foot (2.5 m) head held a huge frill, or bony plate, that curved up and grew as the dinosaur did. But the frill and horns weren't just for show; they were also for defense against predators like Tyrannosaurus rex.

WHO LIVED WHEN?

Dinosaurs lived millions of years ago during the Mesozoic era, which is separated into three time periods: the **Triassic**, the **Jurassic**, and the **Cretaceous**. This diagram shows the periods some of the dinosaurs in this book belonged to. It's easy to imagine they all existed at the same time, but Stegosaurus went extinct 60 million years before Tyrannosaurus rex even existed!

TRIASSIC

251–200 million years ago:
Dinosaurs first appeared

HERRERASAURUS
[230–220 million years ago]

COELOPHYSIS
[225–220 million years ago]

JURASSIC

200–145.5 million years ago:
Dinosaurs ruled Earth

DILOPHOSAURUS
[200–190 million years ago]

APATOSAURUS
[154–150 million years ago]

COMPSOGNATHUS
[161–146 million years ago]

DIPLODOCUS
[155–145 million years ago]

CRETACEOUS

145.5–65.5 million years ago:
Ended when a mass extinction
wiped out dinosaurs

SARCOSUCHUS
[112–110 million years ago]

KRONOSAURUS
[110 million years ago]

SPINOSAURUS
[112–97 million years ago]

GIGANOTOSAURUS
[100–95 million years ago]

BAROSAURUS

[155-145 million years ago]

ALLOSAURUS

[155-144 million years ago]

STEGOSAURUS

[150-144 million years ago]

CORYTHOSAURUS

[80-75 million years ago]

VELOCIRAPTOR

[75-71 million years ago]

PTERANODON

[89-70 million years ago]

EUOPLOCEPHALUS

[99-65 million years ago]

TYRANNOSAURUS REX

[85-65 million years ago]

TRICERATOPS

[72-65 million years ago]

MAJUNGASAURUS

[70-65 million years ago]

an imprint of
■ SCHOLASTIC
www.scholastic.com

Published by Tangerine Press, an imprint of Scholastic Inc.,
557 Broadway, New York, NY 10012
Scholastic Canada Ltd., Markham, Ontario
Scholastic New Zealand Ltd., Greenmount, Auckland
Scholastic Australia Pty. Ltd., Gosford NSW
Grolier International, Inc., Makati City, Philippines
Scholastic UK, Coventry, Warwickshire

Produced by becker&mayer!, LLC.
11120 NE 33rd Place, Suite 101
Bellevue, WA 98004
www.beckermayer.com

becker&mayer!
BOOK PRODUCERS

If you have questions or comments about this product, please visit www.beckermayer.com/customerservice.html
and click on the Customer Service Request Form.

Author: LJ Tracosas
Illustrator: Alex Ries/jupiterartists.com, Colin Howard (teeth illustrations)
Designer: Sam Dawson
Editor: Nicole Burns Ascue and Ruth Austin
Product developer: Peter Schumacher
Production coordinator: Tom Miller

Image Credits—*Sink Your Teeth Into Dinosaurs!*

Front Cover: © Binkski/Shutterstock, © Pinkyone/Shutterstock, © Ratana21/Shutterstock, © Lightspring/Shutterstock; Title Page: © Zepedrocoelho/Shutterstock; Page 2: © ermess/Shutterstock, © Marcio Jose Bastos Silva/Shutterstock, © Maria Arts/Shutterstock, © 2j architecture/Shutterstock; Page 3: © ermess/Shutterstock, © Pinkyone/Shutterstock, © Maria Arts/Shutterstock; Page 4: © ermess/Shutterstock, © hugolacasse/Shutterstock, © fusebulb/Shutterstock, © Marcio Jose Bastos Silva/Shutterstock, © Pinkyone/Shutterstock, © stockphoto mania/Shutterstock; Page 5: © hugolacasse/Shutterstock, © Pinkyone/Shutterstock, © Ratana21/Shutterstock, © stockphoto mania/Shutterstock, © jörg röse-oberreich/Shutterstock, © Catmando/Shutterstock, © Sofia Santos/Shutterstock; Page 8: © fztommy/Shutterstock; Page 16: © tristan tan/Shutterstock; Page 24: © Hein Nouwens/Shutterstock, © Aapthamithra/Shutterstock; Page 34: © Aapthamithra/Shutterstock; Page 38: © ZiaMary/Shutterstock; Page 45: © fztommy/Shutterstock; Page 46: © Binkski/Shutterstock, © Pinkyone/Shutterstock, © kstudija/Shutterstock, © Teguh Mujiono/Shutterstock (3); Page 47: © Binkski/Shutterstock, © Pinkyone/Shutterstock, © kstudija/Shutterstock; Page 48: © Pinkyone/Shutterstock

Design Elements throughout: © Robert Adrian Hillman, © Polina Maltseva/Shutterstock, © pinare/Shutterstock, © Florian Augustin/Shutterstock, © SCOTTCHAN/Shutterstock, © Natykach Nataliia/Shutterstock, © Milagli/Shutterstock, © geographlo/Shutterstock, © OK-SANA/Shutterstock

Printed, manufactured, and assembled in Shenzhen, China, 06/15

10 9 8 7 6 5 4 3 2 1
ISBN: 978-0-545-83131-4

14531